People who have helped the world

HELEN KELLER

by Fiona Macdonald

OTHER TITLES IN THE SERIES
Robert Baden-Powell by Julia Courtney (1-85015-180-6)
Peter Benenson by David Winner (1-85015-217-9)
Louis Braille by Beverley Birch (1-85015-139-3)
Charlie Chaplin by Pam Brown (1-85015-143-1)
Marie Curie by Beverley Birch (1-85015-092-3)
The Dalai Lama by Christopher Gibb (1-85015-141-5)
Father Damien by Pam Brown (1-85015-084-2)
Henry Dunant by Pam Brown (1-85015-106-7)
Mahatma Gandhi by Michael Nicholson (1-85015-091-5)
Bob Geldof by Charlotte Gray (1-85015-085-0)
Mikhail Gorbachev by Anna Sproule (1-85015-218-7)
Martin Luther King by Valerie Schloredt and
    Pam Brown (1-85015-086-9)
Abraham Lincoln by Anna Sproule (1-85015-155-5)
Nelson Mandela by Benjamin Pogrund (1-85015-239-X)
Maria Montessori by Michael Pollard (1-85015-211-X)
Florence Nightingale by Pam Brown (1-85015-117-2)
Louis Pasteur by Beverley Birch (1-85015-140-7)
Eleanor Roosevelt by David Winner (1-85015-142-3)
Albert Schweitzer by James Bentley (1-85015-114-8)
Sir Peter Scott by Julia Courtney (1-85015-108-3)
Mother Teresa by Charlotte Gray (1-85015-093-1)
Desmond Tutu by David Winner (1-85015-087-7)
Lech Walesa by Mary Craig (1-85015-107-5)
Raoul Wallenberg by Michael Nicholson and
    David Winner (1-85015-109-1)

Picture Credits:
American Foundation for the Blind: 5, 10, 11, 13 (right), 42, 50, 53, 56, 57, 59 (top);
Bettmann Archive: 26 (top), 30 (below), 44 (both); Bridgeman Art Library: 4, 12-13;
Culver Pictures: 18, 48; Mary Evan Picture Library: 7, 8, 29; Gamma Presse: 15, 16
(below), 23 (both), 33 (top), 37 (both); Hulton Picture Company: 8-9, 9 (top), 30 (below),
39; Image Select: 47; Images Colour Library: 26 (below); Impact Photos: 58 (top);
Network Photographers: 33 (below); Perkins School for the Blind: 6, 19, 21, 25, 28 (both),
35, 40, 58 (below); Photofusion: 32; Royal National Institute for the Blind: 55; Sense
(National Deaf-Blind and Rubella Association): 16, 54; Science Photo Library: 59 (below);
Telegraph Colour Library: 30 (top).

Special thanks to Alberta Lonergan, Juliet Harlan, Bill Brower and James Clift.

Published in Great Britain in 1992 by
Exley Publications Ltd
16 Chalk Hill, Watford,
Herts WD1 4BN, United Kingdom.

Copyright © Exley Publications, 1992
© Fiona Macdonald, 1991

**A copy of the CIP data is available from
the British Library**

ISBN 1-85015-252-7

Series editor: Helen Exley
Editor: Samantha Armstrong
Picture research: Image Select
Typeset by Brush Off Studios,
St. Albans, Herts AL3 4PH
Printed in Hungary

HELEN KELLER

The deaf and blind woman who conquered her disabilities and devoted her life to campaign for other people

Fiona Macdonald

EXLEY

Freak?

The year was 1920. It was a cold winter afternoon in New York and people were waiting to buy tickets for the performance. Inside, the manager smiled. It was a good audience, better than he had hoped. He'd booked some top-class artistes – tap dancers, acrobats and a troupe of performing seals – but he felt anxious about the new variety act he'd agreed to put on. He'd never had anyone like it in his show before. The New York audiences were keen and quick-witted, but they could also be mocking and very critical. What would they think of his new performers....

The curtain rose. The stage had been arranged to look like a living room. A young man, seated at the piano, rose, bowed, and begged to introduce a stately, dignified, rather elderly woman to the crowded auditorium – Anne Sullivan Macy. Anne made a brief speech. She had a beautiful voice, and was an inspiring speaker. The audience listened, waiting for the real star to appear.

Helen Keller

They did not have to wait long. Anne finished her speech, the orchestra launched into swooping melody, and a tall, elegantly-dressed woman, smiling radiantly, walked on to the stage. Slowly, perhaps a little hesitantly, she made her way over to the piano. Anne took her by the hand, and led her to the middle of the stage, as the audience clapped. Helen stood quietly, while Anne spoke once more to the audience, telling them a story which was heart-warming, touching and yet almost impossible to believe.

Helen took a step forward, still with a brilliant smile, and spread her arms in a wide, embracing

Opposite: The kind of treatment blind people had to suffer: ridiculed and stared at. They were treated as an entertainment, very often in freak shows. But Helen Keller used that very stage to turn people's attention away from mockery and toward taking people with special needs seriously.

Below: Helen Keller in 1920. Even though she could not see herself, Helen took a keen interest in her clothes. Not only did well-made clothes feel nice to wear, but they also conveyed an important message: people with disabilities are entitled to all the good things in life, and should not be content with second-best.

gesture to the audience. Slowly, painfully, haltingly, she began to speak. Every word was a struggle to pronounce, and it was equally difficult for her audience to understand what she was saying. Nevertheless, the New Yorkers sat silent, mesmerized and tense with the effort of concentrating on her words. She spoke only for a little while. When she had finished, there was a storm of applause. In the words of a New York critic, writing in the city's leading newspaper, the audience, one of the most critical in the world, was hers.

Campaigner

The two women were among the most famous Americans of the twentieth century. Anne Sullivan Macy was an educational pioneer, and a brave, uncompromising fighter for what she believed in. Her pupil was Helen Adams Keller who was blind and deaf. She had triumphed over cruel physical disabilities to achieve a brilliant career as a writer, feminist, social activist, and campaigner for people with special needs all over the world.

The text of the speech Helen Keller made, and which so impressed the audience, has survived. Today, some of the words sound rather cloying, but the speech was carefully composed to be in tune with the taste of the times. It also reflects many of Keller's own deepest beliefs – beliefs which gave her the strength and courage to spend many years of her life working to help others.

"What I have to say to you is very simple. My Teacher has told you how a word from her hand touched the darkness of my mind and I awoke to the gladness of life. I was dumb: now I speak. I owe this to the hearts and hands of others. Through their love I found my soul and God and happiness. Don't you see what that means? We live by each other and for each other. Together we can do so much. Only love can break down the walls that stand between us and our happiness. The greatest commandment is: 'Love ye one another'. I lift up my voice and thank the Lord for the love and joy and promise of life to come."

Helen (left) with Anne Sullivan, around 1895. When Helen was "talking" with someone she would put her forefinger and middle finger of her left hand on the person's lips and the thumb on their throat. This enabled her to lip-read and to feel the vibrations of their voice as they spoke. She could then reply at the appropriate moment.

Equality

But what was Helen Keller doing, preaching a "message" like this on the stage? Surely it would have been more fitting to a church, or a political or religious meeting? Quite simply, Helen and her teacher went on stage to earn money. They needed to earn a living. The audiences came, not so much to listen to Helen's message but to gaze at the "living miracle", as she was sometimes known. By the 1920s, the story of how Helen had learned to communicate with other people in spite of her blindness and deafness by "spelling" out words with her hands, was becoming well-known. People who had read about her wanted to see her and to hear for themselves how she had learned to speak. They were curious to look at her, as they might have come to gaze at a rare plant, or at some misshapen animal exhibited as a "freak show" in a fairground.

Left: A poster advertising a "freak show", around 1900. The show was staged by the famous American circus owners, Barnum and Bailey, and toured in France. The poster advertises "tricks and eccentricities of nature", including a telescopic man, a rubber man, a girl with gravity-defying hair, a bearded lady and a Japanese man without arms. Helen Keller was exhibited as a deaf-blind freak with Anne as her assistant.

Above: Rosa and Josepha, Siamese twins (two babies whose bodies have developed joined together in the womb). Siamese twins occur very rarely and do not often survive. They put themselves on display as freaks of nature – a humiliating and inhumane way of living their lives. Helen Keller was reduced to the same situation.

But, at the same time, Helen was making the greatest contribution to improving the position of people with special needs. Helen's achievements and the example that she set were living proof of her capability. She broke through the barriers of prejudice – even if, at times, it meant making a public exhibition of herself – to prove that people with physical or mental problems are capable of living busy, useful, happy and productive lives – just like any other member of the human race. All that is needed is understanding, justice and equality.

Humiliation

It was felt, for many years, that anyone with a physical or mental problem was inferior to so-called "normal" people, and incapable of fully "human" thought. Blind people were made into objects of ridicule – put on stage to perform as clowns, stumbling and falling over objects put in their way – for the amusement of spectators. Others would beg on the streets or outside churches after having been abandoned by their families.

Many people felt embarrassed by the presence of anyone with a disability; Helen's uncle frequently urged her family to "put her away" in an institution,

where she could conveniently be forgotten. Deaf or blind adults were treated like children, sometimes kindly but patronizingly, at other times with this appalling cruelty.

People with special needs

Helen Keller found her work on stage "strange" and tiring. Anne Sullivan hated it. Like many people she found such a public exhibition of disability humiliating. She believed that every individual, whatever physical or mental problems they might have to face, is entitled to be treated with dignity.

Unfortunately, in many countries today, people with special needs are still forced to rely on their families or on private charities for support. They are denied the chance of a suitable education, and, therefore, the opportunity of finding a fulfilling, well-paid job.

However, in certain countries, people with disabilities receive financial support from the state, or are encouraged to find work so that they may lead independent, comfortable lives. Indeed, many people with a medical condition that leads, for example, to blindness or deafness now object very

Above: A blind beggar, asking for money for food and shelter. Helen Keller campaigned to provide training and work opportunities for people with disabilities. She knew that people with disabilities deserved a fair deal from society.

Left: Holding on to one another for guidance, these blind people were forced to live in a workhouse and were treated as outcasts. They would never be employed with their disability and could not, therefore, make a living for themselves or their families.

Helen's father, Captain Arthur H. Keller, taken in the late 1800s. Although Helen was deeply loved by her family they could not reach into her dark, silent existence. They simply tried to make her life more comfortable.

strongly to the word "handicapped". The term "people with special needs" describes their position – and their rights – as members of society with much greater accuracy and sensitivity.

More recently, opinions and, increasingly, the treatment of people with special needs have been changing. Partly, through the work of people in the medical profession, who have made great strides in understanding the causes and management of many medical conditions, even if they are unable to cure them. Partly, through the researches of educational pioneers and psychologists, who study how people learn, and who have therefore, like Helen Keller's teacher, been able to devise teaching methods suitable for pupils who are unable to learn in the usual way. Partly, through the work of charitable organizations, who have campaigned and raised funds to provide better facilities and treatment for millions of people throughout the world. And finally, due to the example set by people with special needs showing what they can accomplish.

Deep South

Helen Adams Keller was born on June 27, 1880, in the small town of Tuscumbia, Alabama, in the Deep South of the United States. Her family was well-established and well-respected in the locality, but, like many Southern gentry at the time, was not very well off compared with the prosperous business tycoons who lived in the bustling Northern cities. However, the Kellers lived a comfortable life with servants, gardeners and grooms employed in their service.

A Southern Gentleman ...

The Kellers owned a large, handsome house, set in luxuriant gardens, and many acres of plantation land. But it was a time of economic depression in the South, following the Confederate defeat in the Civil War, so the Keller plantations did not pay. Instead, Helen's father – Captain Arthur H. Keller – made a living running a small local newspaper, the *North Alabamian.* Even this was not very profitable, and in 1885 he leased it to another company. He had served as an officer in the Confederate army during the war; he was therefore trusted by the Alabama state delegates in Congress who appointed him Marshal – a junior government official – for the northern Alabama district.

Captain Keller was a popular, cheerful, straightforward man, fond of country sports like hunting and fishing. He shared the values of his Southern friends; they liked him because he was a "gentleman" – brave, honest, conventional, courteous, rather lazy (he didn't think it fitting to do hard manual work), a good shot, and good company.

Ivy Green, Tuscumbia, Alabama, USA. An old photograph of Helen Keller's birthplace where she suffered from the illness that left her deaf and blind. Although Helen's campaigns for justice and equality often shocked the local townspeople while she was alive, her house is now a state shrine.

He also shared their appalling racial prejudice. He was reported to have once said, about the black inhabitants of Tuscumbia, "We never think of them as human beings".

A "Memphis Belle"

Captain Keller's first wife died, leaving him with two sons, James and Simpson. In 1875 he married again. His new bride, Kate Adams, was twenty years younger than he was, and came from a prosperous, distinguished and very well-connected Southern family. Kate Adams Keller was much better educated, and probably much more intelligent, than her husband. She had been greatly admired in her home city of Memphis, not only for her good looks (she was tall, with a graceful figure and charming blue eyes) but also for her liveliness, her witty conversation and for her knowledge of books and literature. She was interested in current affairs and was an enthusiastic supporter of votes

for women.

After Memphis, Kate Keller found life in Tuscumbia narrow and dull. Eventually, she came to realize that her marriage had been a mistake, but she remained a hard-working, dutiful and devoted wife. Perhaps it is not surprising that she did not find Captain Keller a very satisfactory companion. He resented her intellectual interests, and grew very angry when she dared to criticize him.

Kate had been brought up in wealthy, rather sheltered surroundings. After marriage, her life changed considerably. Now she had to work hard running the household, cooking meals for the family, preserving fruit and making jam, sewing clothes for herself and for the children, gardening, supervising the servants, caring for her husband and his sons, and, before long, looking after a baby of her own. Somehow, she still found time to read – when she was allowed – to entertain family and friends who came to stay, and to play the gracious hostess to her husband's guests.

Below: The room in the Keller family home where Helen Keller was born in 1880. The wicker basket at the foot of the bed was where Helen slept as a baby.

Left: A cotton plantation in Mississippi, one of the Southern states of the USA. This scene would have been typical of Captain Keller's estate. Black people are hard at work in the fields, while the white owners look on. Slavery was abolished in the USA in 1865, but racial prejudice and economic injustice lingered on.

"The most lively of babies"

Helen was Kate Adams Keller's first child, and Captain Keller's first daughter. She was warmly welcomed into the family, and greatly loved. Captain Keller seems to have been rather sentimental about children, and particularly about his daughter; Mrs. Keller made many of the more sensible, and sometimes difficult, decisions about her upbringing. By all accounts, Helen was a bright, attractive, and very happy baby. She had already learned to walk, and was beginning to learn how to talk, until, in February 1882, when she was only nineteen months old, she was struck down with a sudden, terrifying and mysterious illness.

Those days of illness changed her life for ever.

At first, the family doctor thought Helen would die. She had a high fever, and lay motionless, propped on pillows. No one knows precisely what her illness was. At the time, it was described as "acute congestion of the stomach and brain".

In modern medical terms this is meaningless. Doctors now believe that Helen might have had encephalitis, an inflammation of the brain caused by bacteria or a virus. But the nineteenth-century doctors were right in one respect: Helen might well have died. Even today, encephalitis is regarded as a very serious disease. Treatment with modern drugs and skilled nursing care have improved the chances of survival, but some babies and young children are still not strong enough to fight off an attack.

Dead to the world

Helen survived. Her anxious parents sighed with relief as her temperature returned to normal – the illness left Helen as quickly as it had struck her down. She seemed at last to be free from pain. But relief turned to anguish as they gradually realized how the illness had changed their laughing, lively daughter. She could no longer see them or respond to their voices. Her illness had left her blind and deaf.

From time to time, she still babbled words in

baby-talk, but, since she could not hear her parents' answers or see their lips as they spoke to her, she forgot all the words she had ever learned, except "wha-wah", her word for water.

"Phantom"

Helen's world had been shattered. She was only two years old, but she would always remember her world of silence, darkness and loneliness. She later described how others must have seen her. "Helplessly, the family watched as Phantom's hands stretched out to feel the shapes which she could reach but which meant nothing to her.... Nothing was part of anything, and there blazed up in her frequent fierce anger.... In the same way, I remember tears rolling down her cheeks...."

The happy, loving baby had turned into an isolated, tormented child. In frustration at being totally imprisoned by dark silence, Helen kicked out, bit and pinched people. She broke crockery, stole food from the family's plates, and refused to get dressed. How could they reach into Helen's world? How could they help her and control her? Her family were desperate, what would become of her in the future?

"The way to reach her mind"

In fact, Helen began to help herself. She used her sense of touch and smell – feeling every object carefully, identifying different smells – both inside and outside the house. She worked out a series of signs to indicate what she wanted: to ask for bread she acted out cutting a slice from the loaf and spreading it with butter. A shake of the head from side to side meant "no" and a nod meant "yes". She would push for "go" and pull for "come". Helen was trying to break out.

Her Aunt Eveline urged the family to try to educate her, "This child has more sense than all the Kellers, if there is any way to reach her mind."

It was Helen's mother who discovered the "way to reach her mind". She was reading a book called

Before Anne Sullivan arrived, no one knew how to help Helen communicate with the outside world. Today, children with disabilities are helped by specially-trained teachers, and start learning at a very early age. Here, the large ball helps the baby "feel" sounds through vibrations, as well as providing an enjoyable balancing game.

Above: A teaching session with sensory impaired children involves the whole family. Specialist teachers and parents encourage children to explore their surroundings – in the foreground of this picture, they are concentrating on touching and feeling.
Right: This pen – being used by French children – leaves a raised mark on the paper, so children can feel, with their fingertips, the shapes or letters.

ARBRE

American Notes, written by Charles Dickens, describing his travels in America. One of the places he visited was the great Northern city of Boston. There, he had been very impressed by what he heard of the Perkins Institute for the Blind and its director, Dr. Samuel Grindley Howe. The staff at Perkins had trained another deaf-blind girl, Laura Bridgeman, with great success.

Maybe they could also help Helen?

But Dr. Howe was now dead and, no doubt, his methods had gone with him. However, another great man with an interest in the welfare of deaf-blind people was recommended to Helen's family. He was Dr. Alexander Graham Bell, the scientist who had won international fame as the inventor of the telephone. Bell had devoted his life to teaching and helping deaf people and had married one of his students. All the family used sign language to communicate. Washington, where Dr. Bell now lived, was thousands of miles away from Tuscumbia, but, refusing to be daunted, the Kellers wrote to Dr. Bell, asking for his help. He invited them to call on him in Washington and he put the Kellers in touch with the new principal of the Perkins Institute in Boston, Michael Anagnos, to see whether he could recommend a private teacher for six-year-old Helen.

Miss Sullivan

Anne Sullivan had been a pupil at the Perkins Institute for six years. She was not completely blind, but suffered from repeated ailments which affected her eyes, and often caused her pain. She came from a poor, Irish immigrant family; Anne's mother had died when Anne was only eight years old, and her father was incapable of looking after her as he suffered with a drink problem. With her younger brother Jimmie, Anne was carried off to the state poorhouse, where she lived a nightmare existence among society's "misfits" and "rejects" – adults who were sick, disturbed, involved in petty crime, dependent on alcohol or other drugs, or simply abandoned.

"The most important day I remember in all my life is the one on which my teacher, Anne Mansfield Sullivan, came to me. I am filled with wonder when I consider the immeasurable contrasts between the two lives which it connects. It was the third of March, 1887, three months before I was seven years old."
Helen Keller, from
"The Story of My Life".

Jimmie died in the unhealthy, crowded conditions of the poorhouse, but Anne was "rescued" after flinging herself into the arms of a group of welfare workers, who came to inspect the inmates. They were horrified at what they saw, and hastily arranged to have Anne admitted to Perkins. There, despite clashes with the strict teachers, she did well, and became popular with her classmates.

In 1886, the year the Kellers had taken Helen to see Alexander Graham Bell, Anne was chosen to make a speech on behalf of all the girls who were leaving that year – a mark of great privilege. To Anagnos, young Anne Sullivan – headstrong, determined and bossy, but also brave, sympathetic and highly intelligent – was the obvious choice to send as a teacher to the "phantom" Helen Keller.

"My soul's birthday"

Anne Sullivan arrived in Tuscumbia on March 3, 1887. She was now twenty-one, and Helen was not quite seven. It was a day Helen was to describe later as "my soul's birthday". Before that eventful day, she had merely existed. Now she had begun to learn to live.

It was not an easy process. Helen was wild and quick-tempered, and used only to pleasing herself. Anne realized that Helen would firstly have to learn polite manners and self-discipline, "... obedience is the gateway through which knowledge, yes, and love, too, enter the mind of the child." Without obedience, it would be impossible to teach her anything else. In a letter to her friends, Anne described some of the problems she encountered:

"To get her to do the simplest things, such as combing her hair or washing her hands or buttoning her boots, it was necessary to use force, and, of course, a distressing scene followed. The family naturally felt inclined to interfere, especially her father, who cannot bear to see her cry."

Anne felt determined to reach Helen in spite of the emotional upset it caused both pupil and teacher. One of the first battles for Anne was held in the family dining-room. Seven-year-old Helen

had developed some very bad table manners – helping herself to food from other people's plates and eating everything with her fingers. Anne decided not to let her eat from her plate one Monday morning and a battle of wills began. The rest of the Keller family were so distressed by the scene that followed that they left the room; Anne locked the door and determined to see it through.

Shouting, screaming, kicking, trying to pull Anne's chair from underneath her, poor Helen did not appreciate being told what to do. After a while, when she wasn't getting any reaction from Anne, she quietly went to see what Anne had been doing all this time. She had been calmly eating her breakfast! Helen went all around the table to see who else was there and finding no one, seemed bewildered. After a few minutes she went back to her place and began to eat with her hands.

"When I came to Perkins my life changed a great deal. I could go to school, make friends, and experience many new things. I enjoyed myself more and my motivation and independence increased. Most importantly, I learned to accept my blindness – I learned how much I could do."

*Anindya Bhattacharyya,
a deaf-blind child
from Calcutta, India.*

Anne gave Helen a spoon; Helen threw it on the floor. Anne made Helen get out of the chair and pick it up. She forced Helen to use the spoon and Helen eventually yielded. The same pattern of events then followed with the folding of Helen's napkin. It was an hour later that the two of them left the room with the napkin neatly in its place.

Anne threw herself on to her bed exhausted and Helen went outside into the warm sunshine. A valuable lesson had been learned by both of them. Helen had spirit and determination and Anne had patience and love.

Progress

Anne and Helen made good progress. Helen began to respond to Anne's firm but loving approach. Anne had not been trained as a teacher, but she read all the books she could find on the latest theories of child development. She studied reports of other deaf or blind children. She also wrote regularly to Michael Anagnos, asking for information and advice. Unlike Helen's father, she was prepared to consider Helen's needs rationally, rather than let her emotions cloud her judgment. Sometimes this meant suffering herself (she didn't like seeing Helen in tears, any more than Captain Keller did) in order to do what was best for her pupil.

Perhaps most important of all, Anne thought deeply about how children learn. She watched Helen at play, and remembered all the other young children she had seen, at home, in the poorhouse, and at the Perkins Institute. To her, it seemed as if these children learned best when their lessons arose naturally from activities that interested them. She was not alone in believing this. Around the same time, the great Italian educational reformer, Dr. Maria Montessori, was also teaching children how to "learn through play", with astonishing results.

The Garden-House

Anne quickly realized that Helen would be more receptive to the lessons if she was removed from her family. Captain and Mrs. Keller had always

20

allowed her to do whatever she wanted, whenever she wanted. No one had ever strictly denied Helen anything. A passionate outburst of fury followed every attempt to do so and as Helen grew older, the outbursts became increasingly violent. Anne Sullivan faced a difficult task. "She wouldn't yield to a point without contesting it to the bitter end. I couldn't coax or compromise with her," she wrote to a friend. For the sake of peace Helen had been given her own way throughout her tormented life.

By moving to a little garden-house about a quarter of a mile from the family home, Anne and Helen could work together without distractions. Helen could learn to depend on Anne and to obey her without having her family there to run to when things did not go her way. The house was "a genuine bit of paradise" to Anne, and Helen settled down to living with Anne. She began to pay attention to Anne's spellings on her hand but didn't seem

Helen aged eight, with her dog "Lioness". When Lioness was shot by patrolmen, Helen was grief-stricken. News of Helen's misery was printed in the daily papers, and people from all over the world sent money to buy her a new dog. Determined to help others, Helen said that she would prefer to use the money to help pay for another deaf-blind pupil – a poor boy named Tommy Stringer – to study at Perkins.

sure what they meant. "Helen knows several words now, but has no idea how to use them, or that everything has a name. I think, however, that she will learn quickly enough by and by … she is wonderfully bright and active and as quick as lightning in her movements."

"The Miracle"

Among the first words Anne tried to teach Helen were "doll" and "candy", since these were presents which she had brought with her, and which Helen had obviously enjoyed. Helen copied the signs for these words that Anne made into her hand, and seemed to think this spelling was a game, not yet making the connection between the words and the objects they stood for. But it was early days, and Anne was patient. She taught Helen sewing, crochet, knitting and threading glass and wooden beads to make necklaces. They spent long hours together, exploring Mrs. Keller's garden.

Then, on April 5, 1887, just over a month since Anne's arrival, the hoped-for breakthrough came. Helen learned that everything has a name and that she could learn all she longed to know from the manual alphabet. Helen had been confusing "mug" and "milk" with the verb "drink". One morning Helen wanted to know the name for "water" and Anne saw an opportunity to clear up the child's confusion over what "mug" and "milk" meant, too.

"We went out to the pump-house, and I made Helen hold her mug under the spout while I pumped. As the cold water gushed forth, filling the mug, I spelled 'w-a-t-e-r' in Helen's free hand. The word coming so close upon the sensation of cold water rushing over her hand seemed to startle her. She dropped the mug and stood as one transfixed. A new light came into her face. She spelled 'water' several times. Then she dropped on the ground and asked for its name and pointed to the pump and the trellis, and suddenly turning round she asked for my name. I spelled 'Teacher'."

Helen was overjoyed! "That living word

"Children who hear acquire language without any particular effort; the words that fall from others' lips they catch on the wing, as it were, delightedly, while the little deaf child must trap them by a slow and often painful process. But whatever the process, the result is wonderful. Gradually from naming an object we advance step by step until we have traversed the vast distance between our first stammered syllable and the sweep of thought in a line of Shakespeare."
Helen Keller, from "The Story of My Life".

22

Above: Doctors and teachers have found that regular contact with pets helps those feeling lonely, frightened or isolated to cope with their worries and fears. The donkey provides warmth, trust and something to love. Words are not necessary.

Left: Blind pupils today still learn by using their sense of touch. This girl is studying a row of portrait heads, so that she can "see" what famous people look like.

awakened my soul, gave it light, hope, joy, set it free! There were barriers still ... but barriers that in time could be swept away." For the first time, Helen looked forward to the next day to come.

Breakthrough

From that moment on, Helen never looked back. She was filled with eagerness to learn. Anne reported, "She flitted from object to object, asking the name of everything, and kissing me for very gladness." Within weeks, she knew over three hundred words, and was learning new words at the rate of five or six each day. Because she was busy, and filled with a sense of achievement, she became much happier, and much better behaved. Now she wanted to please, not to fight, the teacher who had opened this "window" of language for her, and set her free from her prison of loneliness.

Anne Sullivan was delighted at her pupil's progress. She also felt rather awed. She wrote, "It is a rare privilege to watch the birth, growth and first feeble struggles of a living mind; this privilege is mine; and, moreover, it is given me to raise and guide this bright intelligence." She spelled words to Helen all day long. Anne realized that we learn to talk by listening to, and copying, the speech of people around us. Since Helen could not listen, Anne would "feed" her mind with words in the only possible way. Here, too, Anne proved herself to be among the most original educational thinkers of her day. Although her teaching methods are commonplace now, at the time, they were new, daring and controversial.

Reading and writing

Within four months of Anne's arrival, Helen could not only recognize and repeat hundreds of words, she was also learning to write. She did this by using a "writing board", developed at the Perkins Institute, which had the shapes of letters cut deeply into its surface. Helen carefully traced each letter onto paper, holding a pencil in her right hand, and guiding its point around each letter-shape with her left-

hand fingertips. Once she had learned to use the writing-board, Helen became a keen correspondent. She wrote to her mother, to the children at the Perkins Institute, and to the principal, Mr. Anagnos. As you can see from her letter, she was also learning to read, using the Braille system:

dear mr anagnos I will write you a letter. I and teacher did have picture, teacher will send it to you. photographer does make pictures. carpenter does build new houses. gardener does dig and hoe ground and plant vegetables. my doll nancy is sleeping. she is sick. mildred [Helen's younger sister] is well uncle frank has gone hunting deer. we will have venison for breakfast when he comes home. I did ride in wheel barrow and teacher did push it. simpson [Helen's step-brother] did give me popcorn and walnuts. cousin rosa has gone to see her mother.

By the age of eight, Helen knew hundreds of words and was able to write and to read in Braille. Following the Braille words (printed in a pattern of raised dots) with her left hand, she would spell out the shapes of each letter in the air with her right hand. The agility of Helen's mind meant that she absorbed more and more information at a rate never seen before in such a disabled child. She was desperate to break out of the silent darkness.

Above: The great
Northern city of Boston,
USA, as it looked when
Helen went there to study
at the Perkins Institute.
Boston was a wealthy city.
The Perkins Institute
relied on gifts from rich
well-wishers to support
pupils like Helen.

Right: Niagara Falls, in the
Great Lakes region which
lies along the border
dividing the USA and
Canada. Here Helen could
feel the drumming of the
water against the rocks and
the spray of the cascading
water against her cheeks.

people do go to church sunday. I did read in my book about fox and box. fox can sit in box. I do like to read in my book. you do love me. I do love you.

good by

Helen Keller

Christmas

Anne Sullivan (whom Helen now called "Teacher", as she was to do for the rest of her life) stayed in the Keller home for the remaining months of 1887.

Christmas that year was a special one for the Keller family and Anne. For the first time Helen took part in all the festivities – in previous years she had remained separate and aloof. She left a stocking out for Santa Claus and opened her presents with excited smiles. Anne had been a blessing to the Keller family and she felt grateful to have been able to reach Helen.

However, Anne sometimes found the Keller family difficult to live with – and they probably felt the same way about her, even though they were profoundly grateful for all that she was doing for Helen. Anne resented any interference with "her" pupil, and it must have been hard, particularly for Helen's mother, to see her daughter becoming ever more closely attached to another person.

"She was awake the first thing [on Christmas morning] and ran to the fireplace for her stocking; and when she found that Santa Claus had filled both stockings, she danced about for a minute, then grew very quiet, and came to ask me if I thought Santa Claus had made a mistake, and thought there were two little girls, and would come back for the gifts when he discovered his mistake."
Anne Sullivan.

Boston

Early in 1888, Anne took Helen to visit Anagnos at the Perkins Institute in Boston. Anagnos was impressed and delighted with Helen's achievements, and captivated by her happy, loving personality. He persuaded Anne to bring Helen to study every now and then at the Perkins Institute, and introduced her to many people who lived in Boston. Soon Helen's progress began to spread all around the United States. She was still only eight years old.

Anne wisely sensed a danger in publicity. She was horrified at the idea of her Helen turning into an "infant prodigy", denied the opportunity of an ordinary childhood, her talents sensationalized

Above: Helen with Michael Anagnos, the Director of the Perkins Institute, which was so advanced in its teaching of blind and deaf children.

Below: Helen with Anne Sullivan in 1890.

and her peace of mind destroyed. Anagnos was not so sure; he hoped that Helen Keller's successes would prove a good advertisement for the Perkins Institute, which had educated Anne as her teacher. Like many other late-nineteenth century thinkers, in his writings, if not in everyday routine, Anagnos saw children as either "angels" or "devils". They were either saintly, uncorrupted beings, "trailing clouds of glory" from their pure, heavenly origins or wicked, selfish creatures, living evidence of all the dangerous instincts buried deep within humanity, needing to be tamed and controlled.

To modern eyes, both views seem unrealistic, but this example of Anagnos's writing about Helen Keller shows that Anne Sullivan's fears of exaggeration were soundly based. "... she is the personification of goodness and happiness.... Of sin and evil, of malice and wickedness, of meanness and perversion, she is absolutely ignorant. She is as pure as the lily of the valley, as innocent and joyous as the birds of the air or the lambs in the field...."

Anne also resented, and rightly so, any suggestion that others had contributed to Helen's transformation. "I have the whole charge of her," she wrote.

"The Frost King"

For the next few years, Helen and Anne divided their time between Boston and Tuscumbia. Helen worked hard at her studies, and enjoyed the wide range of subjects, including French, Latin, and Zoology, that were taught at Perkins.

Relations between Anne Sullivan and Anagnos were often strained, but the final break did not come until 1891 when Helen was eleven. By this time, Helen had begun to write stories of her own, as well as to read hundreds of novels, plays and poems in Braille.

Encouraged by Anne, Helen sent Anagnos a story called The Frost King, which, Anne reported, was all her own work. Anagnos published it in the Institute's annual report, and was horrified to discover that much of the story was from a book by

a well-known writer for children. It seems Helen must have had the book read to her as a young child and had memorized the plot and much of the vocabulary as well. In later years she must have forgotten where the story originally came from. This is not surprising; at Perkins and at home she read so much and worked so hard that many people feared she would overstrain herself, and urged her to rest. Most people accepted this explanation, but Anagnos felt convinced that Anne Sullivan had acted too strongly to support Keller, in order to win praise for her own success with Helen.

Boston, toward the end of the nineteenth century. It was a city of great cultural opportunity – for Helen it was the gateway to her future. The Perkins Institute sent her "Teacher" and gave her many hours of tuition.

Above: Today, teachers adopt the same teaching methods as Anne Sullivan did with Helen Keller: the shape of the mouth, the feel of breath, the vibration of the throat.

Right: Deaf people "listening" to a song with their teeth. Each person holds an "audiphone" – a thin sheet of rubber which vibrates with sound – in front of their mouth. Inventions like this proved to be unsuccessful.

A "living lie"

Even though Anagnos was probably wrong in his accusations that either Anne Sullivan or Helen Keller was "a living lie", his suspicions raised questions that Helen would have to face over and over again, for the rest of Anne's life.

Was Helen really as clever as she appeared, or were some of her achievements faked by her teacher? Were her opinions her own, or was she a mouthpiece for Anne Sullivan's forthright views? Did she work so hard at her lessons because she enjoyed them, or because she was pushed? And was her famous sweetness of character genuine, or an act designed to win friends and sympathizers, who would support her (and Anne) when her family was facing financial difficulties?

Most of Helen Keller's friends and supporters, including Alexander Graham Bell, stayed staunchly loyal. With their financial assistance and encouragement, and with Anne's constant help, Helen continued her studies. In 1894, she and Anne moved to New York, where she attended the Wright-Humason school, which specialized in teaching deaf children how to speak, as well as providing a normal education in academic subjects.

Should she try to talk?

At first, Anne was opposed to Helen learning to talk. She thought it was an insurmountable obstacle; her critics said that it was because she did not want Helen to be able to communicate directly with anyone else. But the impulse to make sound was desperately strong in Helen and, finally, Anne agreed. Anne may have been nervous of allowing Helen to try to speak because of the high chance that she would fail. Most people who are completely deaf are very difficult to understand. Because they can only learn by feeling the lips and throat there is no way that differences in tone can be copied. People who are deaf tend to speak in a flat voice and the words are spoken with very little variety or accent.

Helen made some progress with her speech,

"[Books] tell me so much that is interesting about things I cannot see, and they are never tired or troubled like people. They tell me over and over what I want to know."
Helen Keller.

"The deaf and the blind find it very difficult to acquire the amenities of conversation. How much more this difficulty must be augmented in the case of those who are both deaf and blind! They cannot distinguish the tone of the voice or, without assistance, go up and down the gamut of tones that give significance to words; nor can they watch the expression of the speaker's face, and a look is often the very soul of what one says."
Helen Keller, from "The Story of My Life".

Opposite top and bottom: Reading Braille. The sensitive part of the fingertips is rubbed over each raised dot and space so that the pattern can be interpreted into meaning by the reader. Braille takes up more room than ordinary type so Braille books are bulky and expensive to produce – a further disadvantage for blind people.

Below: A blind typist typing in Braille. He works as part of a co-operative providing jobs for people with disabilities.

and although not everyone could understand her, friends and children could. Her main means of communication at this time were still "spelling" into her conversation partner's hand, plus reading and writing in Braille.

"How splendid it will be ..."

Helen Keller, now fourteen years old, spent almost two years at the Wright-Humason school in New York. It was clear to everyone there that she was an exceptionally intelligent pupil; even though she was not making very good progress at learning how to speak, her written work, particularly in English literature, was admirable.

In 1896, Anne and Helen began to think about studying for a degree. Helen always longed to go to college and was not going to be stopped by her disabilities. Helen wanted to take the entrance exam for Radcliffe College, at that time the most prestigious college for women's education in the United States. Radcliffe had been founded as the "Women's Annexe" of Harvard University; an "annexe" was necessary because male and female students were not allowed to study together at the same institution. Despite the efforts of pioneering women scholars and teachers, the battle for equal opportunities for women to receive an advanced, academic education had still not been won.

Helen knew that preparing for the Radcliffe entrance exam would mean a great deal of hard work, but she was determined to succeed. She had enjoyed all her studies at school and wanted to take them as far as she was able. Typically, she responded to the challenge with optimism and energy, "How splendid it will be ..." she wrote. These qualities – determination, hope and enthusiasm – were perhaps her most characteristic; without them, her life would have been impossible. They also made her a lively and stimulating companion. Throughout Helen's public career, people were attracted by her high spirits and happiness, and by her willingness to try almost anything, whatever the difficulties.

So, in 1896, when Helen was sixteen, both Helen

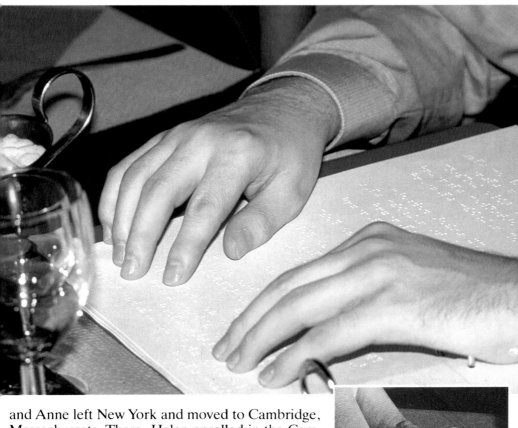

and Anne left New York and moved to Cambridge, Massachussets. There, Helen enrolled in the Cambridge School for Young Ladies, which specialized in preparing pupils to take the Radcliffe entrance exam.

The school was run by Arthur Gilman; he was impressed with Helen's abilities, but felt that it would take her five years to learn all that she needed before going to Radcliffe. She would have to study Ancient History, German, French, Latin, English and Mathematics, all to an advanced level. Some of these subjects, especially advanced mathematics, would be entirely new to her, and, without sight, surely she would find them extremely difficult?

Not for the first time, Anne disagreed with the experts, and encouraged Helen to take the first part of the entrance exam after only nine months. Helen passed, with high marks in English and

German, but Gilman and other friends were worried about the effects of overwork. Helen looked tired and ill, and the strain on Anne was tremendous. The school at Cambridge was designed for pupils with sight and hearing, and, although everyone was extremely helpful to Helen, they were unable to do much to adapt their teaching methods to suit her needs.

Anne attended all Helen's classes, translating the lectures and discussions into "spelling", on Helen's hand. Then, when classes were over, Anne had to spend long hours in the library, reading the books that Helen needed to write her essays and class papers, and translating all the time. While some books had been printed in Braille for Helen to read by herself, many more had not, and so Helen was totally dependent on Anne, and a very few other friends who had learned to spell on Helen's hand, to help her with her studies.

Studying alone

In spite of these difficulties, Anne insisted that Helen would be ready to enter Radcliffe in two years' time. After a bitter quarrel with Gilman, Anne took Helen away from the Cambridge school. They went to live with friends at Wrentham, a small village nearby, and, for the next two years, Helen studied for the final stage of the Radcliffe exams with the help of a private tutor. This move stirred up some of the old controversies – was Anne too protective or too pushy? Did she, rather than Helen, do most of the work? Was she living out her own wish to go to college, rather than serving her pupil's needs?

These accusations worried Radcliffe, and the authorities there were determined to admit Helen only if they could be satisfied about her real intellectual quality. When the time came for Helen to take the final exams, they refused to allow Anne to sit in the room with her and translate the questions on the examination paper. Instead, they had them transcribed into Braille by one of the instructors at Perkins. This time, Helen would have to show what she could achieve, all by herself.

The Radcliffe authorities need not have worried. Even though Helen had some difficulty reading parts of the exam paper (it used a slightly different form of Braille for the mathematical questions than the one she was used to), she achieved good results, with a credit in Advanced Latin. The critics were silenced – and Helen had passed.

Radcliffe – and writing

Helen enrolled at Radcliffe in September 1900, when she was twenty years old. She insisted on following a normal course of study. This meant taking – and doing well in – seventeen-and-a-half courses over several years to qualify for a Bachelor of Arts degree. She specialized in the study of English literature, although she also studied some foreign languages and history. As before, Anne accompanied her to all her classes, and helped her "read" books in the library.

Helen with Anne Sullivan, in 1900. This photo shows the closeness and trust that existed between Helen and her teacher. Helen is sitting with Anne in the tree, even though she cannot see the branch she is sitting on, or the ground below. Helen loved to be outdoors; although she could not see flowers or trees or hear the birds sing, she took great pleasure in the scents and tactile, or touch, sensations of nature.

Helen enjoyed her studies at Radcliffe, but, again, the work proved exhausting. She had little time to make friends with the other young women in her year, or to join them in some of their more light-hearted games and adventures. She and Anne did not live in college, but rented a house nearby. Rather wistfully, she described her college existence as "tedious", adding "my pleasures in what we call college life are few...."

As well as reading, memorizing and absorbing a vast amount of literature while studying at college, Helen also had to write. Since her early days with the writing board and pencil, she had always enjoyed putting her thoughts and feelings down on paper, and had developed a very expressive, direct and immediate style. She wrote good, well-organized essays and clear, simple answers to exam questions, but she found she had another talent.

Author

She was able to explain how she felt about her own condition, about other people's thoughts and actions, and about the state of the world in a way that caught the attention and sympathy of her readers, without sounding gloomy or self-pitying. This impressed one of her college professors so much that he put her in touch with the editor of the *Ladies Home Journal*, a magazine aimed at an educated, middle-class audience, which often printed well-written stories and articles by outside contributors.

The *Journal's* editor was immediately interested. He asked Helen whether she could write the story of her life so far, in five instalments, since he was sure the readers would be fascinated and inspired by all she had managed to achieve. Helen readily agreed, especially since the *Journal* would pay well for her story.

For most of Helen and Anne's life, money was a major problem. Helen's studies at Radcliffe were being paid for by friends, but she did not want to rely on charity for ever. Her father was dead, and her mother had little money to spare. There were no state funds to support her. If charity failed, she

Above and left: Today, blind and deaf people are encouraged to take part in outdoor sports. This requires enormous trust, courage and determination. Horse-riding and rock-climbing are just two of the sports people get involved in. Activities like these were undreamt of before Helen Keller's campaigning. The tremendous progress made in society's attitude to disabled people is due to pioneers like Alexander Graham Bell, Helen Keller and Anne Sullivan.

would have to work or starve. Because she was blind and deaf, many jobs were not open to her, but writing was something she could do. Perhaps the *Journal's* offer would mean the start of a career as a writer.

"A classic"

Once she had embarked on the *Journal* project, Helen soon realized that being a professional writer was not as simple as it looked. She needed help to collect her material and organize her thoughts. A friend suggested that she work with John Macy, a young Harvard graduate who was already working as an editor of a magazine for young people. Macy proved to be tremendously useful; he was intelligent, humorous, well-organized and understood the world of publishing.

With Macy's help, Helen's five articles soon appeared. They were so successful that, with Anne, he urged her to turn them into a book. Helen was reluctant. All this writing was hard work, and she was only half-way through her studies at Radcliffe. She was not sure she had anything new to say. But she realized the need to try and earn money to provide for her future.

Together, Helen, Anne and Macy prepared the manuscript, which contained Helen's own words plus passages by Anne, describing what she had done for Helen. The book, *The Story of My Life*, appeared in 1902, and was widely praised. It was, said the *San Francisco Chronicle*, "full of force, individuality and charm". Macy was convinced that the book would become "a classic", and that it would be read with pleasure for many years to come. It did, and it still is – today it is available in more than fifty languages.

Helen Keller, Bachelor of Arts

Still rather tired, Helen returned full-time to her studies at Radcliffe. She continued to do well, and won the admiration and respect of all her classmates, who recognized that she had to work immeasurably harder than they did. At last, Helen graduated – marked "excellent in English letters" – in the summer of 1904. It was a remarkable achievement, and Helen's friends were very proud of her. What marvel would she achieve next? One friend, Dr. Hale, wrote to her, in a prophetic tone, "... the whole boundless universe is yours."

But was Dr. Hale's prophecy true? Just how many opportunities were really open to someone, like Helen, who was deaf and blind? Helen herself had already recognized the problems, and had spoken out, in a typically generous way, on behalf of all suffering people, in a speech she made to Radcliffe college graduates earlier in 1902.

"There is great work in the world ..." she had said, "there are harsh customs to be made sweet with love; hearts in which a kind, brotherly love must be awakened, time-hallowed prejudices that must be overthrown...." These great causes, rather than the "boundless universe", were what mattered to Helen. For the rest of her life she would concern

Helen at her graduation ceremony when she received her degree from Radcliffe College in 1904. After an enormous effort, Helen had achieved her ambition. But what would she do now? With all her skills and talents, would she still be treated as a second-class citizen because of her disabilities?

herself with trying to right these wrongs. As a friend put it, Helen "inclines to take the side of the people.... She is instinctively philanthropic and benevolent."

Sadly, for Helen, the award of her degree was overshadowed by what she felt to be the unjust ignoring of Anne's contribution to her success. No one at Radcliffe was prepared to make any official acknowledgment of what Anne had done, and both Helen and Anne were deeply hurt by this. Shortly after the graduation ceremony they slipped quietly away, unsmiling, and speaking to no one.

Marriage

But the memory of this miserable event was almost wiped out by another, much more joyful, occasion. In 1905, Anne and John Macy were married. They had fallen in love while they worked together helping Helen with her book. Many people were surprised; Anne was eleven years older than Macy, and completely devoted to Helen. Would she be able to change her life in such a huge way?

An old photograph of Helen (left), John Macy and Anne Sullivan Macy, shortly after Anne and John were married. Here, the three friends are discussing a page of manuscript, perhaps from one of Helen's books. While John Macy helped Helen with her books his own were not particularly successful. Although Helen welcomed John into the close friendship she shared with Anne, his marriage to Anne was unsuccessful.

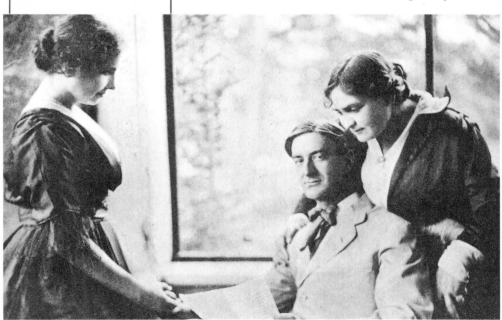

At first, Anne herself doubted that it would be possible, but she was very much attracted by Macy, and, perhaps, longed for the chance to be loved for herself alone, and not in her role as friend and teacher. Outwardly, Helen shared in Anne's happiness. She exclaimed when she heard the news: "It is almost as wonderful as if I was going to be a bride myself. I would have been miserable if you had not accepted him."

It is impossible for us to tell, at this distance, what these remarks really meant. Perhaps Helen was being unselfish and tactful, wishing to spare Anne any worries about how she might react to this surprising piece of news. Perhaps she was genuinely delighted to share in Anne's hopes for the future. Or perhaps her remark tells us just how much she had come to see the world from Anne's point of view.

Probably the truth lies somewhere in between. Certainly, Anne, Helen and Macy must all have realized that their lives would change very considerably as a result of this marriage. Helen herself said frequently at this time that she would never marry, even though many of her older friends, including Alexander Graham Bell, urged her to do so. She was young, bright, pretty, friendly, sympathetic and lively, yet, because of her difficulties with communication, she could not believe that any man would love her. "I should think it would seem like marrying a statue," she said.

Threesome

While *The Story of My Life* had not been a runaway best-seller, it had provided Helen and Anne with enough money to buy a house in Wrentham. Here they hoped to settle and to make a living by writing and occasionally lecturing, although, for the moment, they were still supported by charitable funds. John Macy came to live with them there. He, too, was working as a writer, but did not make enough money to contribute significantly to the household's living expenses. At first, all three were very happy. Macy joked, talked, helped them with their writing – they had received commissions for

"I want people to understand that deaf-blind people are not so different. We use our minds the same way sighted, hearing people do. We have goals and dreams just like they do. Deaf-blind people have a lot to offer.

"We want to be treated the same as other people. Sure we need help to do some things but everyone needs help sometimes. We want what we can do to be recognized."

Anindya Bhattacharyya,
a deaf-blind child
from Calcutta, India.

other books and articles – and did odd jobs, like making shelves to store all Helen's books, around the house. He cleared a "safe" area in the large gardens where Helen could walk by herself, without having to ask other people to lead her by the hand.

Public service and public affairs

The American people had followed Helen's life story with admiration and curiosity for many years. Whether she, and Anne, liked it or not, Helen was a public figure. Helen's concern for people with impaired sight or hearing – or who were suffering in any other way – was also well known. In 1906, Helen, now twenty-six, received the first of many invitations to sit on public committees, and to act as a spokesperson for blind people. The state of Massachusetts was one of the first to set up a Commission for the Blind, and Helen was one of its first members. She played an active part campaigning for better treatment and opportunities for ·blind people. In particular, she felt that blind people should be offered the chance to work, if at all possible. Charity was a fine thing, but how much more dignified to be able to support yourself, and to show people that even though you were blind, you were not stupid or incapable.

Helen also hit the headlines with her campaigns on another issue related to blind welfare. Doctors had discovered that many babies were being born with a serious eye infection caused by a sexually-transmitted disease. If untreated, this infection led to permanent blindness, and yet could easily be cured by drugs administered shortly after birth.

Treatment was not always given, since people – doctors and nurses among them – did not like to admit that "nice" mothers might have sexually-transmitted diseases. Information about the sight-saving treatment therefore remained largely unknown. It seems hard to believe that modesty and prudishness could lead to so many children suffering unnecessarily for the rest of their lives. To Helen, it seemed outrageous, and she was determined to join with others – including many early feminists –

Opposite: A portrait photograph of Helen, taken in 1908, when she was twenty-eight. Helen gave this photo to Onorio Ruotolo, a sculptor who was carving a statue of her. As a "modern heroine" – and an attractive woman – Helen was a popular subject for photographers and artists.

"She [Helen Keller] will live on, one of the few, the immortal names not born to die. Her spirit will endure as long as man can read and stories can be told of the woman who showed the world there are no boundaries to courage and faith."

Senator Lister Hill of Alabama, USA.

Above and right: Helen Keller devoted her life to supporting causes – not only for the rights of disabled people but for strikers and for women's equality. Her popularity and fame ensured publicity for these causes and she "used" that power to get minority groups noticed and accounted for by society.

who were trying to break the taboo. She made a point of mentioning the issue whenever she had an audience, even in the most polite circles and on public platforms. Eventually, the message got through, and many babies' sight was saved.

The Red Flag

John Macy brought many changes to the household at Wrentham when he married Anne. At this time, Helen was increasingly determined to spend time helping the people who did not get reasonable treatment from society. As yet, she had remained largely uninvolved with party politics, although she had followed with interest the struggles of women in England and America to win the vote. In her journal she recorded comments on burning political issues of the day; these reveal that she regularly sided with the poor and oppressed, although her preference was always for peace, rather than conflict and bloodshed.

Helen's political inactivity was largely because she had few contacts with people who held liberal or progressive views similar to her own. Most members of her family were traditional in their social and political opinions. Anne, while not active in political affairs, was also conservative, although she disapproved of the racial prejudice she found in the Southern states. In contrast, Macy, like many other intellectuals at the time, was deeply involved in the Socialist movement, and he introduced Helen to Socialist ideas, publications and people.

In 1909, Helen became a member of the American Socialist Party, and, assisted by Macy and, to a lesser extent, Anne (who was following her husband), joined enthusiastically in many of its campaigns. They supported a pioneering strike of textile workers at Lawrence, Massachusetts, organized by the Industrial Workers of the World (IWW) movement. Later Helen became friendly with two of the IWW leaders. She proudly displayed a red flag, the symbol of Socialist workers' rebellion, on the wall of her study, and sent for copies of a German workers' newspaper, which was printed in Braille.

"At another time she asked, 'what is a soul?' 'No one knows,' I replied; 'but we know it is not the body, and it is the part of us which thinks and loves and hopes … [and] is invisible....' 'But If I write what my soul thinks,' she said, 'then it will be visible, and the words will be its body.'"
Anne Sullivan, 1891.

She wrote essays and articles on Socialist topics, which were collected together and published as a book in 1913.

People first

Helen's support for the workers' strikes, and for other radical causes, including abolishing the death penalty and prohibiting the employment of young children, made her unpopular with many American citizens. This was not the pure, unsullied "lily of the valley" that Michael Anagnos had praised. Should heroines concern themselves with the sordid world of murder, poverty, hunger and work?

People were even more shocked and scandalized when Helen spoke out for the campaign to make birth control readily available to all women, especially to poor women struggling to raise children on an inadequate income. Helen also caused consternation among her friends and relatives in the Southern states when she gave her support to the National Association for the Advancement of Colored People, who were demanding full civil rights for all black people throughout the United States.

Helen supported both these causes for humanitarian reasons. She wanted fairness, compassion, justice and love to replace inequality, privilege and neglect. As a woman who was totally dependent on others for all her everyday needs, she recognized the importance of independence for women – in work, at home and in their family lives. And as a member of a dependent and disadvantaged minority group, she supported the demands of another minority to seek freedom and equality in the eyes of the law.

She also felt guided by her religion. For many years, she had followed a branch of the Christian faith known to its followers as the "New Church", but more commonly referred to as Swedenborgism, after its founder, Emanuel Swedenborg, who lived during the eighteenth century. Helen's commitment to this religion was a real sign that she was developing independent opinions for herself; her family had been Presbyterian and Anne Sullivan was a Roman Catholic. In a letter written to a newspaper,

"I believe that life is given to us so we may grow in love, and I believe that God is in me as the sun is in the color and fragrance of a flower – The Light in my darkness, The Voice in my silence."

Helen Keller.

46

Helen explained:

"The New Church ... fosters all kinds of true freedom, places humanity above party, country, race, and it never loses sight of Jesus's gospel – the supreme and equal worth of every human soul...."

The fight for peace

In the years 1914-1918, war devastated Europe, with Britain, France and Russia fighting against Germany and its allies. America was sympathetic to the British cause, but remained neutral. However, as the war progressed, the American president, Woodrow Wilson, became convinced that he must intervene in support of Britain and her allies.

Many Americans, including Helen, were opposed to the brutality of war, and demanded peace, rather than an extension of the conflict. In particular, Helen pointed to the vast amounts of money being spent on guns and other equipment to arm the American soldiers. How much better it would

be, she argued, if all that money could be spent peacefully, to help poor, sick or disabled people instead.

This campaign for peace, which was organized by International Workers of the World, was almost the last political issue with which Helen openly became involved. She decided that, in future, she could best help the cause of blind and deaf people by keeping her party political views to herself. She still maintained her strong beliefs in equality, peace and social justice, but from now on, most of her public statements were carefully phrased and designed not to offend any potential giver to the causes for which she worked.

Separation

Helen was busy, active and happy, involved in her political and humanitarian campaigning. But all was not well at home. In 1913, John Macy had walked out of the house at Wrentham. Anne was living through a time of anger, anxiety and fading hope. The marriage was over, said Macy. He and Anne could not get on, and he could not live as part of a threesome. Bitterly, he said he should have realized that when he was marrying Anne, he was marrying an institution. Anne could not, would not, be a "real" wife. Always, he complained, Helen had to come first. Anne was tired, bad-tempered, and unpredictable. He had had enough.

Anne was devastated. Sorrowfully, Helen recorded, "She kept demanding my love in a way that was heartbreaking. For days she would shut herself up almost stunned, trying to think of a plan that would bring John back or weeping as women who are no longer cherished weep." She tried to bring about a reconciliation, and wrote repeatedly to Macy, assuring him that he would be welcomed back, and that Anne's moodiness was caused by the strain of a lifetime spent caring for someone else.

Macy would not come back. He went to live in New York, where he continued to try to make a living as a writer. Helen and Anne still helped him, from time to time, with gifts of money. It seems

Helen dancing with Polly Thomson. On a well-made wooden dance floor, Helen could feel some of the music's beat through the soles of her shoes. Helen enjoyed Polly's lively company as Anne grew increasingly ill and unable to care for Helen.

that Anne went on loving him for the rest of her life, in spite of the anguish and bitterness of their separation. She refused ever to consent to a divorce.

Lecturing

At the same time that Anne's marriage was collapsing, she and Helen were also hard at work on a new project, designed to try and make money. They set off on a series of lecture tours, which aimed to tell educated, professional and charitable audiences just how Anne had helped Helen to learn, and how the education of other blind or deaf children might also be improved. They received a fee for each lecture, plus expenses, and sometimes there was a collection for charity as well. It was exhausting, if ultimately worthwhile, work, and took them away from home for several months at a time.

Polly Thomson

Anne, in particular, found these lecture tours extremely tiring. She was almost fifty years old, and no longer strong; she had repeated attacks of the eye disease that had troubled her since childhood, and had become unhealthily overweight. Wisely, she decided that it was time to train someone to help her look after Helen. In 1914, Anne chose Mary Agnes ("Polly") Thomson, a young Scot, to be Helen's assistant and housekeeper. Polly was to remain with Helen for the rest of her life. At around the same time, a young socialist sympathizer, Peter Fagan, was recruited to act as Helen's secretary.

In 1916, Anne became seriously ill. Tuberculosis was diagnosed, and she was ordered to rest, and to seek a warm climate. She needed a complete break, with no worries, for several months. But just before Anne left for a break, there was a brief, tragic interlude: Helen fell in love. For a long time Helen had felt that marriage was not for her. However bravely she claimed the right to equality within society, and however proudly she proved herself through her academic achievements, she was sometimes troubled by doubts as to whether she was capable of getting married. She knew that she wanted to love and to be loved, but did she have the right to expect any man to put up with her disabilities?

Love

But now, in 1916, here was a man who claimed that he loved her just as she was, and that he wanted to spend his life with her. This unexpected admirer was Peter Fagan, her new secretary. She had already come to like and respect him – he was quiet, efficient, discreet and trustworthy. He obviously cared enough for her to have learned the "spelling" language used by Anne, and how to read Braille, as well. They shared radical Socialist views. Helen was astonished, but secretly delighted. This is how she described his proposal:

"I was surprised that he cared so much about me. There was a sweet comfort in his loving words. He was full of plans for my happiness. He said if I would marry him, he would always be near to help me.... His love was a bright sun that shone upon my helplessness and isolation. The sweetness of being loved enchanted me, and I yielded to an imperious longing to be part of a man's life...."

They decided to get married. Helen was now thirty-six, and an accomplished, famous woman, but she still feared her family's reaction. She knew they would not approve of Fagan's Socialist views. He was also younger than her – at the time of his proposal, he was twenty-nine – and an employee. They tried to keep their engagement a secret, and planned to elope, but one of the servants told Anne.

She immediately contacted Helen's mother, who, as Helen predicted, did everything she could to try and stop the marriage. Anne had to go into hospital, and Helen was taken back to her sister Mildred's home in Alabama, where her widowed mother now lived. She was kept there, under strict supervision, as if she had been a naughty child.

Courage

Fagan made several attempts to come and see her, bravely standing up to Mildred's husband, who was brandishing a gun. Helen was equally courageous, hiding out on the porch all one night, waiting for Fagan to come and meet her, to lead her away to a new life. How she found her way there, in a strange house with a heavy suitcase, remains unknown. But Fagan never came; probably he was stopped on his way by Mildred's husband and his servants, who were looking for him, and fled in fear of his life. After that, Helen seems to have decided that it was too dangerous to try and escape. The couple agreed to wait for a better opportunity, but to keep in touch by letter.

Meanwhile, Helen's family tried very hard to make her change her mind. Eventually, they succeeded, and Peter Fagan played no further part in Helen's life. As Helen explained, the violence of their feelings killed her love for him. "The unhappiness I had caused my dear ones produced a state of mind unfavorable to the continuance of my relations with the young man." Very sadly, she also wrote that she eventually accepted this as part of her destiny, "I came to believe that marriage was to be denied to me, like music and sunshine."

Why?

Why did Helen's family stop her marrying a kindly, scholarly, helpful, hard-working young man? Was it just his Socialist principles and his junior position, or was there some other reason? Did they, perhaps, share Helen's feelings that, because of her physical difficulties, she ought not to marry? Did they feel that Helen was somehow too precious and extraordinary to settle for a normal domestic life? Did they cling to her unreal childhood image of saintly purity, in spite of all her involvement with feminist and Socialist causes? Or did they feel that Anne's unhappy marriage had shown that the two women would not be able to live happily together if either of them were closely involved with a man? We do not know. What we do know is that Helen remembered Peter Fagan for the rest of her life, and looked back on his love as "a little island of joy, surrounded by dark waters."

"Some people are scared to approach a blind person, or talk to us or make friends. What are they scared of? We're not going to punch them out! They're not going to go blind if they touch us! We're just as human as they are, except we can't see!"

From "Are The Stars Out Tonight?" by Jim Morse.

Problems

As always, Helen displayed remarkable energy and resourcefulness in coping with difficulties and disappointments that would have crushed many other people. She determined to put her unhappy experience of love to good use, "I faced consciously the strong sex-urges of my nature and turned that life energy into channels of satisfying sympathy and work." Anne had by now recovered, and the two women, cared for by Polly Thomson, went back to the lecture circuit.

This made some money, but it was obvious that, as a way of life, it could not go on for ever. They went to Hollywood to make a film about Helen's life, called *Deliverance*, which was completed in 1918, and, in 1920, decided to go on the stage. At first, the financial rewards were considerable, but by 1924, prospects again looked bad. Anne's health was failing, Helen was not making much money

Helen, Anne Sullivan and Polly Thomson with Charlie Chaplin in Hollywod, USA, in 1918. During the making of Helen's film, "Deliverance", Chaplin explained the filming process, while Anne translated his words into "spelling" on Helen's palm.

> *"When we do the best we can, we never know what miracle is wrought in our life, or in the life of another."*
>
> *Helen Keller.*

Helen's work as an "ambassador" made many people realize just what could be done to help blind people lead full lives, working and relaxing like everyone else. Simple innovations, like this floating board, have enabled thousands of blind people to learn how to swim in safety.

from her writing, the lecture tours had stopped and the stage bookings were few and far between. They sold the large house in Wrentham, and moved to somewhere smaller and cheaper to run. To pay the bills, they relied on the pension (of $5,000 a year for life) given to Helen by the millionaire philanthropist, Andrew Carnegie, and on other gifts from well-wishers.

"A national asset"

Fortunately, the president of the newly-founded American Foundation for the Blind, Major M.C. Migel, approached Helen with a suggestion: would she, as probably the best-known blind woman in the world, help them to raise funds? Would she also help them in their campaign to improve the public awareness of the needs of blind people, and teach the American people about the skills blind people had to offer, and the important work they would do?

Of course, Helen said yes. For the next thirty

years, Helen was actively involved with the Foundation. She gave hundreds more lectures, spoke at innumerable luncheon and dinner parties, attended fund-raising receptions all over the United States, shook hands with presidents and politicians, doctors, church leaders, teachers and journalists. All the time she acted as an "ambassador" for blind people, presenting a lively, intelligent, capable and, above all, normal image to the public, and doing everything she could to dispel centuries of fear,

Helen's lifestyle – she lived in her own home, and not in a hospital or institution – showed that people with disabilities could lead independent lives. This blind girl is preparing a meal for herself and her family.

misunderstanding and prejudice.

In return, the Foundation cared for her. Migel said he regarded her as a "national asset", and arranged for the Foundation to pay her for all the work she did on its behalf. He also gave generously from his own wealth, and persuaded other families to do the same. For the first time in her life, it seemed as if Helen would be financially secure.

"The Guardian Angel of the Blind"

Helen's work brought her, and all people with special needs, increasing respect. In 1932, *The Pictorial Review* gave her its annual prize for the "most noteworthy contribution by a woman". This was a real mark of distinction. She was awarded honorary degrees by American universities. Publishers asked her to write more books and articles, and she had been introduced to an adept and sympathetic editor, Nella Braddy Henney, who would help her with almost everything she wrote.

Helen's work with the Foundation also led her, once again, into politics, but this time it was different. Now she was working as the representative of a large charitable organization, asking the government to make major changes in the services provided to help blind people in every state. In 1935, after an intensive lobbying campaign, the American Federal Government finally agreed to include the blind in the list of people with special needs incorporated in a new Social Security Act. Now, blind people would be entitled to some measure of help from the state. Unlike Helen, they would not have to depend entirely on their families, or on charity.

Helen photographed next to an early radio, 1932. Helen could "listen" to radio music through her fingertips which had become incredibly sensitive to vibrations. She also made a broadcast – on The Radio Home Makers' Club – heard throughout the United States.

Anne Sullivan's death

Helen enjoyed her busy life; she knew she was working well, and helping people. But her happiness was overshadowed by worry. Anne had just turned seventy and was ill and tired. Now she, too, was almost blind. Together, Helen, Anne and Polly spent time away together which they hoped would build up Anne's strength. Bravely, Anne fought against her growing weakness – "I am trying so hard to live for you," she said – but on October 20, 1936, she died. Helen had Polly to help her, and many kind and willing friends, but no one could possibly replace Anne Sullivan Macy. She was a woman of great character, skill and devotion. She had generously given her whole life to helping Helen Keller. How would Helen survive without her?

Life without Anne

To help blot out her grief, Helen decided to travel overseas. She had received many invitations to visit blind people in other countries, and to inspect the services and facilities provided for them. With Polly, she decided to visit Japan, and their trip was a great success. Crowds came to greet her, and she was received as an important guest. On their return to America, she and Polly moved into a new, purpose-built home, given to her by a wealthy benefactor, and settled down to the familiar routine of writing, lectures and meetings.

World War II

In 1939, war broke out in Europe. Again, America was neutral at first, but for Helen Keller further travel overseas was obviously impossible. After the bombing of Pearl Harbor in 1941, America joined in the war. Helen's pacifist conscience was horrified, and, as before, the tragic waste of life and resources sickened her. But she was outraged by the Japanese attack on American ships, and appalled by news of the Nazi atrocities in Germany. What could she do, to show her sympathy for the casualties of war, to help those "less fortunate" than herself, without seeming to support violence? She would visit newly-blinded Americans in hospital, to comfort and encourage them. Helen's example of what a severely-disabled person could accomplish helped many injured people; she called these hospital visits "the crowning experience of my life."

Later, Helen went to Europe to share her experiences with staff of the American Foundation for

Helen and Polly visiting wounded American soldiers during World War II. The lives that many soldiers faced after crippling shell-fire seemed bleak and terrifying. Helen visited the wounded and gave them inspiration – she was living proof of the joys and achievements that could still fill their lives.

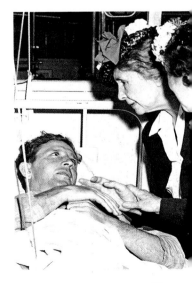

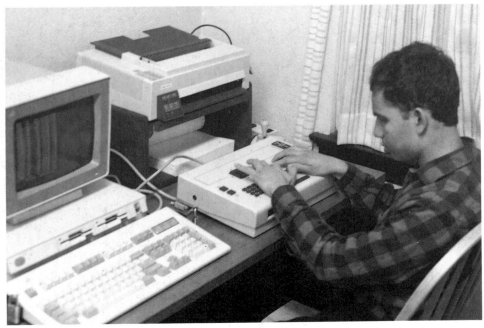

Left: Helen Keller aged eighty – still reading Braille and still beautifully-dressed.
Opposite top: A victim of river-blindness – a disease caused by a parasite living in tropical waterways. Blindness can be caused by many different things, but Helen Keller showed that it need not debilitate people's lives completely.
Opposite below: Anindya Bhattacharyya is a pupil at Perkins Institute. He was born in Calcutta, India. Here, Anindya types on a Versa-Braille machine. He is determined to show the world that he has as much to offer as any able-bodied person.
Below: A guide-dog of the future? This computerized robot called "Meldog" has been developed in Japan.

the Overseas Blind, who were helping with the many military and civilian casualties left behind in war-torn Europe. She also returned to Japan, and visited the devastated cities of Hiroshima and Nagasaki, where American planes had dropped the world's first atomic bombs. She pledged, there and then, "to fight against the horrors of atomic warfare and for the constructive uses of atomic energy."

During this tour, Polly Thomson became ill, and she and Helen had to return to America. Helen's friends were increasingly anxious. Unlike Anne, Polly had refused to train anyone else to look after Helen. She lacked Anne's greatness of heart, and Anne's intelligent, unselfish care for her pupil. Polly's devotion was total, but narrow and more possessive. On this occasion, Polly recovered, and she and Helen resumed their travels. In 1951, they went to South Africa. The Zulu people called Helen "Homvuselo" – "You who have aroused the consciousness of many". In 1952 they went to the lectured extensively within the United States. Their next trip was to India, then back again to Japan.

On all these journeys, Helen continued to ask questions, gather information, give interviews and make friends. Aged seventy-five, she was still working hard to show the world just what blind people could achieve. Many of the changes implemented overseas to help those with special needs can be traced back to Helen Keller's visits.

Old age

Polly Thomson died in 1960. From now on, Helen was cared for by her secretary and her nurse. The close, protective circle of people who had known and loved her was growing smaller, but Helen continued to visit friends, to read, and, in a restricted way, to enjoy her life. In 1961 she suffered a slight stroke, and this diminished her ability to communicate with the people around her. For the rest of her life, she was almost as isolated as she had been before Anne arrived to change her world.

Helen Adams Keller, aged eighty-eight, died at home, peacefully, in 1968. She was buried in America's National Cathedral, in Washington DC, a reflection of her great achievements and position as one of the most loved and respected women of the early twentieth century. She had triumphed against tremendous difficulties to bring hope, dignity and a measure of justice to people with special needs in America and beyond.

These triumphs had been won through faith, courage, determination, and sheer hard work. Sometimes, the costs to Helen herself had been high; sometimes, the pressures of fame, frustration, loneliness and sense of "difference" must have been hard to bear. With Anne Sullivan Macy's help, Helen Keller learned how to communicate; it was her own sense of purpose, and her own wish to help, that made her decide how to live. On her eightieth birthday, newspaper reporters asked her what plans she had for the future. Her reply was characteristic: "I will always – as long as I have breath – work for the handicapped."

"They took away what should have been my eyes, (But I remembered Milton's Paradise). They took away what should have been my ears, (Beethoven came and wiped away my tears). They took away what should have been my tongue, (But I had talked with God when I was young). He would not let them take away my soul – Possessing that, I still possess the whole."

Helen Keller.

Important Dates

1880   June 27: Helen Adams Keller is born in Tuscumbia, Alabama.

1882   Helen falls ill, aged only nineteen months. She loses her sight and hearing and, eventually, speech.

1886   Captain Keller, Helen's father, takes Helen to Washington to meet Dr. Alexander Graham Bell. He contacts the famous Perkins Institute in Boston.

1887   March 3: Anne Sullivan arrives as a private tutor to teach Helen.

1888   Helen, now eight years old, and Anne go to Boston, where Helen visits the Perkins Institute and meets its director, Michael Anagnos.

1889-91   Helen studies partly at home, partly in Boston. Anne quarrels with Anagnos.

1891   The "Frost King" scandal.

1894   Helen and Anne travel to New York, where Helen studies at the Wright-Humason school.

1896   They move to Cambridge, where Helen prepares for the Radcliffe College entrance exam at the School for Young Ladies, run by John Gilman. Helen becomes interested in the Swedenborgian branch of the Christian faith.

1897   Anne quarrels with Gilman; she and Helen leave his school and go to live in Wrentham. Helen studies with the help of a private tutor.

1889   Helen passes the entrance exam to Radcliffe College; the authorities there are satisfied that her academic achievements are genuine, and that she has not been unfairly helped by Anne.

1900   Helen, aged twenty, attends Radcliffe College.

1902   *The Story of My Life* is published.

1904   Helen graduates with a Bachelor of Arts degree from Radcliffe.

1905   Anne Sullivan and John Macy are married.

1906   Helen is invited to become a member of the Massachusetts State Commission for the Blind.

1909   Helen joins the Socialist party, and takes part in many political and humanitarian protests, including campaigns for female suffrage, birth control and civil rights. She also continues to write.

1913   John Macy and Anne's marriage ends with John leaving. Helen and Anne go on lecture tours to try to earn money.

1914   World War I breaks out and continues until 1918.
        Polly Thomson joins Helen and Anne.

1916   Peter Fagan falls in love with Helen. They become engaged, but Helen's mother and sister stop the marriage.

1918   Helen, Anne and Polly go to Hollywood, to make a film based on Helen's life. The critics like it, but it is not a financial success.

1920   Helen and Anne work in stage shows.

1924	Helen starts to work for the American Foundation for the Blind, helping to raise funds and acting as a "goodwill ambassador". She also takes part in lobbying campaigns to improve state welfare benefits for blind people.
1927	Helen writes more books, now with the help of Nella Braddy Henney.
1930	Anne becomes seriously ill. She travels abroad with Helen and Polly.
1931-35	Helen and Anne are awarded honorary degrees and other prizes. Major Migel, of the American Foundation, calls Helen "The Guardian Angel of the Blind".
1936	Anne Sullivan dies.
1937	Helen and Polly travel to Japan.
1938	Helen moves to a new, purpose-built house in Westport, Connecticut, where she makes many new loyal, helpful and sympathetic friends. She continues to work for the American Foundation for the Blind.
1939	World War II breaks out and continues until 1945. The United States joins the war in 1941 when the Japanese bomb Pearl Harbor.
1943	Helen visits newly-blinded soldiers and sailors in American military hospitals.
1946	Helen and Polly visit Europe on behalf of the American Foundation for the Overseas Blind.
1948	They travel to Australia, New Zealand and Japan, meeting blind people.
1951	Helen and Polly visit South Africa.
1952-57	They travel to the Middle East, Latin America, Scandinavia, India and Japan.
1960	Polly Thomson dies.
1961	Helen becomes ill, and gradually loses contact with the outside world.
1968	Helen Keller dies, aged eighty-eight.

"Helen Keller's courage and her achievements have helped professionals and parents, as well as educators, rehabilitation specialists, and government officials recognize the ability and potential of every handicapped person to live as a productive and contributing member of society."

Kevin J. Lessard, Director of the Perkins Institute, 1989.

Glossary

Bacteria (singular: bacterium): One kind of microbe – microscopic organisms that are too small to be seen with the naked eye.

Braille: The system of writing for blind people that was devised by Louis Braille. It uses six dots to express the entire alphabet, punctuation and mathematical signs. The dots are raised out of the flat surface of paper.

Civil War: In America, the war that started in 1861 between the Southern (Confederate) and Northern (Union) States over States' rights, in particular the issue of slavery. The Southern States wanted slavery to continue, while the Northern States wanted it abolished. The war ended in 1865 with the total defeat of the Southern States.

Confederate: The Confederate States of America that was formed during the American *Civil War*, when eleven Southern (Confederate) States broke away from the United States. These States – Alabama, Arkansas, North Carolina, South Carolina, Florida, Georgia, Louisiana, Mississippi, Tennessee, Texas and Virginia – were reunited with the USA when the war ended.

Congress: The national law-making body of the USA. It is made up of the Senate and the House of Representatives.

Encephalitis: Inflammation of the brain, caused by *bacteria* or a *virus*.

Nazi: A member of the National Socialist German Workers' Party, which was founded in 1919 and seized power in 1933 under Adolf Hitler.

Philanthropist: Someone who shows concern for the well-being of humanity, usually by making charitable donations.

Prodigy: Someone who has exceptional talents or qualities.

Psychologist: A person who studies the human mind and the way it functions.

Sign language: Visual gestures that are used mainly by deaf or dumb people as a means of communication.

Socialist: A supporter of socialism, a system of social organization which advocates that the means of production and distribution of goods should be owned and controlled by the community as a whole, rather than by private ownership.

Tuberculosis: An infectious disease that, most often, attacks the lungs. Symptoms include coughing, spitting blood and loss of weight.

Swedenborg, Emanuel (1688-1772): A Swedish scientist, thinker and religious writer. He started having visions and from 1747 devoted the rest of his life to spiritual research and writing. He never preached or established a religious sect and wanted his teachings to be spread through existing churches. However, inspired by his writings, his followers founded the New Jerusalem Church in 1788.

Virus: The smallest known microbe, much smaller than a *bacterium*.

Zoology: The scientific study of animal life.

Index